Koinōnía

AUTHENTIC FELLOWSHIP

BIBLE STUDY GUIDE

From the Bible-teaching ministry of

Charles R. Swindoll

Published by

INSIGHT FOR LIVING

Post Office Box 4444
Fullerton, California 92634

Distributed by

WORD
Educational Products Division
Waco, Texas 76796

These studies are based on the outlines of sermons delivered by Charles R. Swindoll. Chuck is a graduate of Dallas Theological Seminary and has served in pastorates for over twenty-two years, including churches in Texas, New England, and California. Since 1971 he has served as senior pastor of the First Evangelical Free Church of Fullerton, California. Chuck's radio program, "Insight for Living," began in 1979. In addition to his church and radio ministries, Chuck has authored twenty books and numerous booklets on a variety of subjects.

Chuck's outlines are expanded from the sermon transcripts and edited by Bill Watkins, a graduate of California State University at Fresno and Dallas Theological Seminary, with the assistance of Bill Butterworth, a graduate of Florida Bible College, Dallas Theological Seminary, and Florida Atlantic University. Bill Watkins is presently the director of educational resources, and Bill Butterworth is currently the director of counseling ministries at Insight for Living.

Creative Director:	Cynthia Swindoll
Editor:	Bill Watkins
Associate Editor:	Bill Butterworth
Copy Supervisor:	Wendy Jones
Editorial Assistants:	Becky Anderson and Julie Martin
Communications Manager:	Carla Beck
Communications Coordinator:	Alene Cooper
Art Director:	Ed Kesterson
Production Artists:	Becky Englund and Donna Mayo
Typographer:	Trina Crockett
Calligrapher:	Richard Stumpf
Cover Designer:	Michael Standlee
Cover:	Painting by Arthur J. Elsley, *Golden Hours,* reproduced by courtesy of the Medici Society, London, England; Graphic Arts Unlimited, Inc.
Production Supervisor:	Deedee Snyder
Printer:	R. R. Donnelley & Sons Co.

An album that contains eight messages on four cassettes and corresponds to this study guide may be purchased through Insight for Living, Post Office Box 4444, Fullerton, California 92634. For information, please write for the current Insight for Living catalog, or call (714) 870-9161. Canadian residents may direct their correspondence to Insight for Living Ministries, Post Office Box 2510, Vancouver, British Columbia, Canada V6B 3W7, or call (604) 669-1916.

Table of Contents

1. This message was not a part of the original series but is compatible with it.

Koinōnía
Authentic Fellowship

In a world that places a premium on independence, it's easy for us to conclude that "going it alone" is a sign of strength—even in our Christian walk. But we really do need each other. God made us that way! In His family we are interrelated . . . fellow members of the Body of Christ. Our lives are to touch others deeply.

The Bible calls this "fellowship." The Greek term is koinōnía. *This is the word the early Christians used to describe the bond that held them together. It wasn't a shallow, meaningless pat on the back. It was an authentic display of love and acceptance, care and compassion, support and forgiveness—all those things that characterized the Lord Jesus Christ when He walked on earth.*

These messages do more than announce what ought to be. They also deal with how to do it and why it is so important.

If you are interested in the horizontal dimension of Christianity . . . if you hunger for more than an isolated relationship with Christ . . . if you really want your faith to be something shared instead of just declared, koinōnía awaits you!

Chuck Swindoll

Putting Truth into Action

Knowledge apart from application falls short of God's desire for His children. Knowledge must result in change and growth. Consequently, we have constructed this Bible study guide with these purposes in mind: (1) to stimulate discovery, (2) to increase understanding, and (3) to encourage application.

At the end of each lesson is a section called **Living Insights.** *There you'll be given assistance in further Bible study, thoughtful interaction, and personal appropriation. This is the place where the lesson is fitted with shoe leather for your walk through the varied experiences of life.*

It's our hope that you'll discover numerous ways to use this tool. Some useful avenues we would suggest are personal meditation, joint discovery, and discussion with your spouse, family, work associates, friends, or neighbors. The study guide is also practical for church classes and, of course, as a study aid for the "Insight for Living" radio broadcast. The individual studies can usually be completed in thirty minutes. However, some are more open-ended and could be expanded for greater depth. Their use is flexible!

In order to derive the greatest benefit from this process, we suggest that you record your responses to the lessons in a notebook where writing space is plentiful. In view of the kinds of questions asked, your notebook may become a journal filled with your many discoveries and commitments. We anticipate that you will find yourself returning to it periodically for review and encouragement.

Bill Watkins
Editor

Bill Butterworth
Associate Editor

Koinōnía

Authentic Fellowship

Koinōnía
Acts 2:44–47

When we sail through the waters of Christian truth, we can stay close to the shoreline where the currents are mild and the waves manageable, or we can venture out to sea where the currents are stronger and the personal risks greater. In this series, we are going to lift anchor and steer our ships into the potentially dangerous yet rewarding waters of Christian *koinōnía*. Our voyage will have its perils—the most threatening of which will be personal sacrifice and involvement in the lives of others. But such are the risks of genuine Christianity. If you are ready for an adventure, then grab your Bible and climb aboard. We are about to discover the scriptural treasure of authentic fellowship.

I. The First-Century Saints.

As we flip through the pages of the New Testament, we witness the birth and hear the first cries of the infant Church delivered by God. The Christian Church came into existence a few years prior to 40 A.D. It began when the Holy Spirit descended with power on the apostles who were gathered together on the day of Pentecost (Acts 2:1–4). The multitudes who saw this event heard the Apostle Peter explain what had happened. He declared to them that what they had witnessed was a sign of a brand new work begun by God among both Jews and Gentiles (vv. 14–36). Peter went on to tell them how they could be forgiven of their sins—a proclamation that led to about three thousand of them accepting Jesus Christ and being baptized in His name (vv. 37–41). What these new believers initiated immediately after their conversion displays their deep commitment to, and fellowship with, one another. The text gives us the four main ingredients of the communion they enjoyed: "And they were continually devoting themselves to the apostles' teaching and to fellowship, to the breaking of bread and to prayer" (v. 42). Let's briefly examine each of these practices in the order that they are explained in the biblical record.

1

A. Teaching. The instruction these baby Christians were given came from the apostles, who in turn received their information from the Lord Himself. The apostles' teaching was authenticated by miracles that God performed through them (v. 43b). As a result of all of this, "everyone kept feeling a sense of awe" (v. 43a).

B. Fellowship. The kind of communion the new believers enjoyed was that of mutual sharing. The Book of Acts recounts what they did: "And all those who had believed were together, and had all things in common; and they began selling their property and possessions, and were sharing them with all, as anyone might have need" (vv. 44–45). These activities were not communistic or socialistic. They were engaged in voluntarily, and the goods shared were not distributed evenly but given to meet needs as they arose (cf. Acts 4:32, 34–35; Philem. 14; 1 Pet. 5:2).

C. Eating. We read that "day by day continuing with one mind in the temple, and breaking bread from house to house, they were taking their meals together with gladness and sincerity of heart" (Acts 2:46). These young Christians ate together frequently. And when they did, they expressed joy and showed authenticity toward one another.

D. Prayer. Their gatherings were marked by prayers of praise (v. 47a). They knew not only that the Lord had saved them but that He would also sustain and encourage their growth. Therefore, they raised their voices toward heaven and gave Him the thanks and honor that was due Him.

II. The Twentieth-Century Saints.

Passing through time from the first century into the twentieth, we come to the contemporary scene of the local church. As we scan the landscape and peer into the doors of theologically conservative churches, we find solid teaching, frequent eating, and habitual prayer times. But one key ingredient is conspicuous by its absence— koinōnía, authentic Christian fellowship. We're not referring to social events intended simply for our entertainment. Rather, we are speaking about the saints' sacrificial giving to one another. In order to understand this more clearly, let's probe further into the meaning of biblical fellowship and then take a look at some of its most basic constituents.

A. The Meaning of Koinōnía. We can draw three truths about koinōnía from Acts 2 that will help us accurately define it. First, *Christian fellowship included all believers* (v. 44). No distinctions or discriminations were to be made (cf. Gal. 3:28). Of course, no

2

one was forced to gather with other Christians, but the opportunities were available for those who wanted to participate. Second, *Christian fellowship held believers together* (Acts 2:44). It promoted unity in the midst of diversity (cf. 4:32a). And third, *Christian fellowship met the needs of believers* (2:45). It was not designed to be just another gathering, but its purpose was to provide help for those Christians who needed it. In a word, New Testament koinōnía was *sharing*. Given these facts, Christian *koinōnía* may be defined as "expressions of genuine Christianity freely shared among the members of God's family." This idea of sharing has at least two aspects. We can share something *with* someone—such as money, words of encouragement, confessions of failure, or statements of need. And we can share *in* something with someone—such as a sorrow, a joy, or an area of mutual concern.

B. **Some Constituents of Koinōnía.** Now that we have an idea about what is meant by Christian fellowship, let's investigate some of its most essential elements.

1. **Love and Acceptance.** In the strictest biblical sense, *ágápe* love involves seeking the greatest good of the other person. At times, this may include giving reproof, encouragement, instruction, or even an embrace. But whatever the means of expression, the attitude conveyed is one of value and respect for the other individual. This requires tolerance and understanding, not prejudice and disinterest.

2. **Honesty and Humility.** Of course, love and acceptance cannot flower without genuine expressions of honesty and humility. Truthful vulnerability and a servant's heart are crucial factors of authentic koinōnía.

3. **Concerns and Restoration.** The Apostle Paul's words on this are quite clear: "Brethren, even if a man is caught in any trespass, you who are spiritual, restore such a one in a spirit of gentleness; each one looking to yourself, lest you too be tempted. Bear one another's burdens, and thus fulfill the law of Christ" (Gal. 6:1–2). When other Christians struggle over, wander away from, or simply fail to keep God's directives, our primary goal should be to lovingly help steer them back on course. Obviously, we cannot do this for each other if we are silent about our needs and deaf to the cries of those around us.

4. **Confession and Forgiveness.** In an atmosphere of love, acceptance, honesty, humility, and concern, wrongs can be freely confessed and graciously forgiven. And although sharing about sins committed can seem threatening, failure to confess them can delay sought-after healing (James 5:16).

5. **Encouragement and Availability.** Some local assemblies have become known as places where human spirits are criticized and demoralized. However, the biblical exhortation is that churches be composed of believers who "stimulate one another to love and good deeds" by "encouraging one another" toward this goal (Heb. 10:24–25).

6. **Informality and Flexibility.** The rut of the routine and the highly structured can be fatal to koinōnía. There is nothing wrong with procedures and programs as long as they facilitate rather than hinder the spiritual development of God's people.

III. **Some Timely Questions.**

Reflecting on what we have learned about koinōnía so far, there are several questions that we could ask ourselves. Among these, three stand out. Seek to answer them honestly. Your responses will reveal how well you are practicing the art of Christian fellowship.

A. **Am I seeking Christian fellowship or forsaking it?**

B. **Do I provide an atmosphere conducive to sharing and encouraging or to guarding and criticizing?**

C. **Am I sensitive and flexible enough to meet others' needs when they arise, or am I so hard and unbending that I just pass the needy by?**

Living Insights

There are at least six characteristics of koinōnía that we focused on in this lesson. Let's delve into them further by zeroing in on some more biblical passages that deal with these traits. Copy the following chart into your notebook. Then look at the Scriptures listed and jot down some observations on each of the qualities of Christian fellowship.

Koinōnía	
Traits	Observations
Love and Acceptance Ephesians 3:17–19, Romans 12:9–16	
Honesty and Humility Ephesians 4:14–16, 25	
Concerns and Restoration Galatians 6:1–2	
Confession and Forgiveness James 5:16	
Encouragement and Availability Hebrews 10:23–25	
Informality and Flexibility Hebrews 13:1–3	

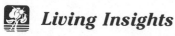 *Living Insights*

Do you remember *pretests* from your elementary school days? Usually on a Monday the teacher would give a quiz to see how many spelling words you could write correctly *before* going over them throughout the week. Let's do the same for your knowledge about koinōnía. Copy the following chart into your notebook and fill it in with what you know about each of these areas before we study them together.

Love and Acceptance

_____

_____

_____

Honesty and Humility

_____

_____

_____

Concerns and Restoration

_____

_____

_____

Confession and Forgiveness

_____

_____

_____

Encouragement and Availability

_____

_____

_____

Informality and Flexibility

_____

_____

_____

Koinōnía: Love and Acceptance
1 Corinthians 13:1–5a

As we discovered in the last lesson, *koinōnía* means "expressions of genuine Christianity freely shared among the members of God's family." This cannot occur without love and acceptance. In fact, when these qualities are absent, saints become snobs and selflessness is replaced with selfishness. Koinōnía needs the fertile soil of Christian love in order to take root and bloom as God intends. Recognizing this truth, we need to take some time in God's Word to understand His perspective on love. And among the numerous passages we could turn to, perhaps none is more definitive than 1 Corinthians 13:1–7. These verses are so saturated with important material on the subject of love that we have chosen to concentrate on a portion of them here and the remainder in the subsequent lesson. Before moving on, let's commit ourselves to being open to the surgery these words can perform in our lives. For unless we allow them to penetrate our minds and wills, we run the risk of never enjoying the many benefits of fellowship that God longs to give us.

I. The Priority of Love.

The very structure of the opening comments in 1 Corinthians 13 alerts us to love's all-important status in God's sight. Let's take some time to gain an appreciation for the arrangement and message of the first three verses.

A. The Conditional Clauses.
The word *if* introduces five statements that refer to either a spiritual gift or a sacrificial action.

If I speak with the tongues of men and of angels . . .
(1 Cor. 13:1a; cf. 12:10b, 2 Cor. 12:2–4)
If I have the gift of prophecy, and know all mysteries and all knowledge . . .
(1 Cor. 13:2a; cf. 12:8, 10a)
If I have all faith, so as to remove mountains . . .
(13:2b; cf. 12:9a)
If I give all my possessions to feed the poor . . .
(13:3a; cf. 12:28b, where the word *helps* is a synonym for *giving*; Rom. 12:8a)
If I deliver my body to be burned . . .
(1 Cor. 13:3b; cf. Dan. 3:13–18)

B. The Contrastive Statements.
Three times, the phrases that start with *if* are put in opposition to the clause "but do not have love" (1 Cor. 13:1b, 2c, 3c). If we were to summarize the thought

of this passage so far, we might state it in these words: "If I had the spiritual gifts of tongues, prophecy, wisdom, knowledge, faith, and giving, and performed great acts of self-sacrifice, but was unloving . . ."

C. The Concluding Remarks. Completing each contrastive sentence is a phrase that delivers one of three conclusions to the argument. The first closing remark tells us that speaking in tongues without love is equivalent to saying nothing of value (v. 1c). The second one informs us that possessing the gifts of prophecy, wisdom, knowledge, and faith without love reduces one's life to nothing of value (v. 2c). And finally, we are told that giving liberally of one's goods and sacrificially of one's life without possessing love brings the giver nothing of value (v. 3c). We can summarize the instruction given in these verses with the following statements:

1. If I do not have love, my *words* are empty.
2. If I do not have love, my *life* is empty.
3. If I do not have love, my *gains* are empty.

Love is so significant that its absence reduces life to zero!

II. The Meaning of Love.

The word *love* occurs throughout 1 Corinthians 13 and is translated from the Greek term *àgápe*. It means "seeking the greatest good of another person." The idea this word conveys is that an individual who has àgápe love will long and strive for the best interests of others. This is the highest kind of love that a person can possess. In fact, the Scriptures reveal that God *is* àgápe love (1 John 4:8b), which puts this love on a supernatural plane. Thus, no human being can produce or attain it. Only the One who is love can cause it to become a reality in our lives. But we might ask, What are the characteristics of this love that put it out of our natural reach? The answer to this lies in 1 Corinthians 13:4–7. Here we discover fifteen attributes of àgápe love. Let's look at the first seven qualities in this lesson. We will delve into the remainder of them in the next study.

A. Love is patient (1 Cor. 13:4a). Genuine love does not have a short fuse, no matter how unreasonable or unfair people may be. Rather, love is slow to express irritation or anger (cf. James 1:19–20).

B. Love is kind (1 Cor. 13:4a). A person who possesses a loving spirit renders gracious, helpful service to others. He or she is friendly, free from petty criticism, and slow to condemn (cf. John 8:2–11).

8

C. Love is not jealous (1 Cor. 13:4b). People who have àgápe love do not burn with envy for the possessions of others. Neither do such individuals vigilantly guard their own property from being used by others. Instead, loving persons are glad for those who have received greater prosperity, rank, and/or abilities than they, and are willing to share what they have.

D. Love does not brag (1 Cor. 13:4b). Authentic love does not engage in ostentatious boasting. Vain and presumptuous words and actions do not accompany true expressions of love. However, love does graciously accept appreciation and reward for deeds performed, but it does so without drawing undue attention to itself.

E. Love is not arrogant (1 Cor. 13:4c). Individuals who have love do not strut around with inflated egos (cf. 4:6–7). Rather, they make accurate assessments of their strengths and weaknesses and refuse to belittle someone who has not achieved or received as much as they.

F. Love does not act unbecomingly (1 Cor. 13:5a). It is not characterized by shameful, rude behavior. Instead, it seeks to take the proper action at the best time and in the most loving way. In a word, it is tactful.

G. Love does not seek its own (1 Cor. 13:5a). Unloving people demand that their rights be observed, require that their ways be followed, and insist that their interests be satisfied above anyone else's. On the other hand, people who have love yield their rights, ways, and interests when others will be benefited. In other words, selflessness, not selfishness, is a hallmark of love.

III. The Vulnerability of Love.

After looking at these qualities of love, it's not difficult to see that true love includes an open, unguarded approach to other people. But that's a scary concept for most of us to deal with. After all, vulnerability can set us up to be hurt and maligned. Doesn't it make more sense to keep our barriers raised until we are assured that a personal attack is unlikely? In fact, why take any risks at all? Why not protect ourselves behind walls that no human being can penetrate? Certainly this approach would eliminate almost any potential for being wounded by another person. It would also separate us from the many joys and benefits of both human and divine love. In short, if we want the advantages of love, then we must be willing to take the risks of love. And that requires vulnerability. Of course, we can refuse this path and trod another one devoid of openness. But the toll on such a road is extremely high. As C. S. Lewis so graphically put it:

There is no safe investment. To love at all is to be vulnerable. Love anything, and your heart will certainly be wrung and possibly be broken. If you want to make sure of keeping it intact, you must give your heart to no one, not even to an animal. Wrap it carefully round with hobbies and little luxuries; avoid all entanglements; lock it up safe in the casket or coffin of your selfishness. But in that casket—safe, dark, motionless, airless—it will change. It will not be broken; it will become unbreakable, impenetrable, irredeemable. The alternative to tragedy, or at least to the risk of tragedy, is damnation. The only place outside Heaven where you can be perfectly safe from all the dangers and perturbations of love is Hell.[1]

1. C. S. Lewis, *The Four Loves* (New York: Harcourt Brace Jovanovich, Inc.), p. 169.

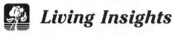 *Living Insights*

Koinōnía begins with love and acceptance. Yet with all the talk about love, it's amazing how few people really understand what it is! Let's do some further study in 1 Corinthians 13.

● The chart below contains the first seven characteristics of love found in 1 Corinthians 13. Copy it into your notebook and then review your notes. Look for the basic definition of each term and expand on it in your own words. Finally, jot down some other passages that address these specific traits.

Characteristics of Love (Part One)		
Love . . .	Expanded Definitions	Additional Scriptures
Is Patient		
Is Kind		
Is Not Jealous		
Does Not Brag		
Is Not Arrogant		
Does Not Act Unbecomingly		
Does Not Seek Its Own		

Living Insights

The purpose of the second "Living Insights" is to provide us with an opportunity to apply the truths we learn. So as you work through this study, think about how these characteristics of love manifest themselves in your life.

- Let's do a little self-assessment. Make a copy of the following chart in your notebook. Think through your ability to love. Next to each characteristic, write down your personal strengths and weaknesses. Then commit to the Lord through prayer the areas in your life that need improvement.

Characteristics of Love in My Life (Part One)		
Love . . .	Personal Strengths	Personal Weaknesses
Is Patient		
Is Kind		
Is Not Jealous		
Does Not Brag		
Is Not Arrogant		
Does Not Act Unbecomingly		
Does Not Seek Its Own		

Koinōnía: Love, Sweet Love

1 Corinthians 13:5b–7; Romans 12:10, 15:7

A number of years ago, Hal David and Burt Bacharach teamed up and composed a song that in part said this:

Lord, we don't need another mountain.

There are mountains and hillsides enough to climb.

There are oceans and rivers enough to cross . . .

enough to last 'til the end of time.

What the world needs now is love, sweet love;

No, not just for some but for everyone. . . .

It's the only thing that there's just too little of.[1]

How true is this message! And it is just as applicable to Christians as it is to non-Christians. In fact, we could change the chorus to say, "What the *Church* needs now is love, sweet love." More than anything else, the Body of Christ is to be characterized by sacrificial love. Jesus said so when He spoke these words: " 'A new commandment I give to you, that you love one another, even as I have loved you, that you also love one another. By this all men will know that you are My disciples, if you have love for one another' " (John 13:34–35). As Christians, our desire and goal should be to flesh out this directive on a daily basis. But what does this involve? How can we do it? Let's turn once again to God's Word in order to find sound answers to these practical questions.

I. Love in General.

Before we continue to examine the specific facets of love found in 1 Corinthians 13:5b–7, let's look at two passages that speak about love in general between believers.

A. Romans 12:10. This verse explains that the love Christians have toward one another should be marked by devotion and unselfishness. The dedication we have to our spiritual family should exhibit the same loving qualities that are often shared among natural family members. And the esteem that we grant to fellow believers should be for their direct edification, not our indirect exaltation.

B. Romans 15:7. Here Christians are exhorted to "accept one another, just as Christ also accepted us to the glory of God." The Greek word translated *accept* was frequently used in two distinct ways during the New Testament era. First, this term was

---

1. "What the World Needs Now Is Love." Words by Hal David and music by Burt Bacharach (New York: Blue Seas Music, Inc.; Jac Music Co., 1965).

employed with reference to welcoming a person into one's home, thus conveying the idea of hospitality. Second, the word was used in the context of a person being assigned to a military unit. When a soldier was inducted into a certain outfit, he was generally received with a spirit of comradery. In other words, love between believers is not genuine unless it is accompanied by visible expressions of selfless acceptance.

II. Love in Particular.

In our last lesson we explored several attributes of love given in 1 Corinthians 13:4–5a. There we discovered that love is long-suffering, helpful, generous, humble, tactful, and selfless. In this study, we are going to complete our analysis of love and consider how we should respond to our findings.

A. Love is not provoked (1 Cor. 13:5b). Genuine love does not allow irritability or bitterness to creep in and mar its motivation or expression. Instead, love looks beyond a person's sins and reaches out to meet his or her needs (cf. James 5:20, 1 Pet. 4:8).

B. Love does not take into account a wrong suffered (1 Cor. 13:5c). The Greek word for *take into account* was an accountant's term used in the first century. It means "to credit or place into someone's account." The idea in this context is that love does not record or store up wrongs committed against it. Unexpressed resentments over offenses suffered will lead to a torturous existence filled with bitterness and devoid of love (cf. Matt. 18:21–35). In such an atmosphere, koinōnía cannot thrive, much less exist. Forgiveness must occur before fellowship can be experienced.

C. Love does not rejoice in unrighteousness (1 Cor. 13:6a). Christian love neither finds pleasure in nor sympathizes with the wickedness done by others. Instead, love is wounded and grieved when sin performs its work of destruction (cf. Eph. 4:29–31).

D. Love rejoices with the truth (1 Cor. 13:6b). Love and truth are close companions. Indeed, one cannot exist without the other. When people sincerely love one another, they are honest and open about their thoughts and feelings. Of course, truth spoken in love can sometimes be difficult to handle. But as an ancient sage once said,

> Faithful are the wounds of a friend,
> But deceitful are the kisses of an enemy.
> (Prov. 27:6)

It's better to be bruised by the trustworthy words of a caring friend than to be flattered by the deceitful compliments of a self-serving foe.

E. **Love bears all things** (1 Cor. 13:7a). The word for *bears* means "to cover" so as to protect, shield, or support something. This term was frequently used to describe a warrior's use of his shield as an instrument of protection. Given this, the word presents the idea that real love withstands the blows and attacks of others. For example, love is not offended when acts of kindness go unappreciated. One person's love for another is not ruined when his or her friend relates a secret to a third party that had been communicated in the strictest confidence. A relationship glued by love does not suffer irreparable damage when an act of giving is not reciprocated in kind. Love is not fickle or conditional. Neither is it easily hurt or hindered.

F. **Love believes all things** (1 Cor. 13:7b). This verse does not mean that love is gullible or undiscerning. Rather, it means that love is trusting—not suspicious, cynical, or narrow. Love gives people the benefit of the doubt and makes every allowance for their failure.

G. **Love hopes all things** (1 Cor. 13:7b). True love anticipates and seeks the best in others. It never gives up; it operates with an incurable confidence in God's ability to change people.

H. **Love endures all things** (1 Cor. 13:7c). Love has the determination and courage to press on even when facing humanly insurmountable obstacles. In short, love refuses to quit and retreat. Instead, it stands patient and tough against the storms of life.

III. Our Response.

Without Christian love, there can be no Christian fellowship. With authentic love, koinōnía will not only occur, but it will become the witness to the world that God intended it to be (John 13:35). Given this, how should we respond to the biblical teaching on love?

A. **"I'm never going to be unlovely again."** That's a nice commitment, but it will never last. We cannot express supernatural love by drawing simply on our natural powers.

B. **"I have tried it and failed, so I have concluded that it isn't worth the effort or the risk."** This response contradicts the repeated biblical imperative we have been given to love one another.

C. **"I admire the qualities of love, but alone I can't produce them; so Lord, produce them through me as I submit to You."** These are the words that God is waiting to hear. Do you want love to characterize and flood your life? Then rely upon God to create the changes in you as you seek to obey His directives. Because He *is* love, He will not disappoint you (1 John 4:7–8, 15–16).

Living Insights

First Corinthians 13 tells us what love is all about. We began our work on this subject in the last study. Let's wrap it up by looking at the remaining eight traits.

- The following chart can be added to the one from the previous study or copied separately. Draw from your notes a definition of each trait and then list some additional passages that amplify its meaning.

Characteristics of Love (Part Two)		
Love ...	Expanded Definitions	Additional Scriptures
Is Not Provoked		
Does Not Take into Account a Wrong Suffered		
Does Not Rejoice in Unrighteousness		
Rejoices with the Truth		
Bears All Things		
Believes All Things		
Hopes All Things		
Endures All Things		

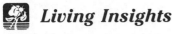 *Living Insights*

Is your life characterized by love? Let's continue our self-evaluation.

- The following chart can be added to the one given in the previous lesson. Next to each trait write in both your strengths and your weaknesses. Then thank God for your stronger points, and ask Him to help you improve some of your weaker ones.

Characteristics of Love in My Life (Part Two)		
Love . . .	Personal Strengths	Personal Weaknesses
Is Not Provoked		
Does Not Take into Account a Wrong Suffered		
Does Not Rejoice in Unrighteousness		
Rejoices with the Truth		
Bears All Things		
Believes All Things		
Hopes All Things		
Endures All Things		

Koinōnía: Honesty and Humility
Luke 22:7–14, 23–24; John 13:1–17

Few people would disagree that the world needs to be changed. However, not many would agree on what alterations should take place and how they ought to be accomplished. These issues are debated even among believers. Some Christians think that significant changes can best be brought about when God's people gain control in the political arena. Others maintain that the most effective way to prompt change in people is by administering the gospel electronically through the mass media. But when we study the methods Jesus used to alter lives, we find a very different approach. Sure, He spoke to large crowds on occasion. And yes, He addressed political leaders from time to time. However, during His earthly ministry, He invested much of His time in the lives of just twelve men. Of these, eleven went on to change the world by preaching the gospel and ministering to people. They had learned from their Master (1) that the transformation of the world depends on the transformation of individuals and (2) that neither process can occur without God's involvement. Furthermore, the disciples were instructed by Christ that honesty and humility were required in order for needed changes to occur in the members of God's family. Without these qualities, genuine koinōnía cannot exist. The Lord made this point in a number of ways. Perhaps the most graphic way is recorded in John 13:1–17. Revealed in these verses are six principles concerning honesty and humility. They can help transform us into more godly individuals if we will only take the necessary steps to apply them in our relationships with others.

I. Some Essential Background Material (Luke 22:7–14, 23–24).

We will understand and appreciate the teaching in John 13 more fully when we become familiar with some crucial elements of its historical setting.

A. The Passover Meal. Luke tells us in the Third Gospel that prior to Christ's betrayal and crucifixion, Jesus and His disciples made preparations to celebrate the Passover. This was an annual event that had occurred in Jewish homes since the days of Moses (Exod. 12:1–20). It was designed to remind the Jews of how the Lord had graciously and mightily delivered them from Egyptian bondage. As a result, the Passover was looked upon as a permanent memorial of God's faithfulness and redeeming power. The Passover meal involved preparing and consuming an unblemished, year-old, male lamb, unleavened bread, and bitter herbs (vv. 3–6, 8). When the time had come for Jesus and His disciples to celebrate it together for the last time, the Lord sent out Peter and John with some instructions. He told them to find a certain man carrying a pitcher of water, follow him to his home, and upon arriving there, prepare the Passover meal (Luke 22:7–12). Peter and John did exactly what Jesus requested and found everything just as He said they would (v. 13). After all the preparations had been made, Jesus and His disciples reclined together at the table (v. 14). In Christ's day, this usually involved sitting or lying on the floor around a wooden table where the food was set out.

B. The Specific Disputes. After they had gathered for the memorial meal, the disciples "began to discuss among themselves which one of them" would betray Christ (v. 23). "There arose also a dispute among them as to which one of them was regarded to be greatest" (v. 24). In short, the disciples tried not only to exonerate themselves before one another but also to exalt themselves in each other's sight.

C. The Foot-Washing Custom. The attitudes behind the disciples' squabbling were accentuated by the fact that they had failed to wash their feet before coming to eat the Passover meal. This was a significant omission, for in Jesus' day roads were not usually paved. Thus, feet covered only by sandals became quite soiled as they walked the dirt roads. Because of this, homes usually had large water pots sitting outside their doors for the purpose of cleansing people's feet before they came inside. If a household had a servant, then he or she would wash the feet of those who came. If there was no servant, then a family member or even a guest would graciously assume the foot-washing task. But at their last meal together, not one of Jesus' disciples performed this job. Apparently, they were so caught up in their own egos that they refused to serve one another by washing each other's feet.

II. Some Relevant Principles on Honesty and Humility (John 13:1–17).

With this background material before us, we are now ready to extract from John 13:1–17 six lasting truths about being transparent with others and having an accurate assessment of ourselves. The context of this passage is Jesus' final Passover meal. And His washing of the disciples' feet is the event it records.

A. Honesty and humility must be prompted by love (v. 1).
We are told that "before the Feast of the Passover, Jesus knowing

that His hour had come that He should depart out of this world to the Father, having loved His own who were in the world, He loved them to the end [that is, to the utmost]." Even when Christ was facing an excruciating death, He continued to love His disciples to the maximum. He never failed to say and do whatever was in their best interest. This involved both truthfulness and selflessness on His part. Indeed, a nonjudgmental honesty and a genuine humility can only flow from a person who deeply cares for others.

B. Honesty and humility need no announcement (v. 4). After Jesus had reclined at the dinner table with His disciples, He "rose from supper, and laid aside His garments; and taking a towel, He girded Himself about." The Lord knew that His followers had come to the meal with dirty feet. He also realized that their bickering over who would betray Him and who was the greatest among them could not go unaddressed. Jesus could have stood in their midst and said, "Now I want to demonstrate true humility to you." But this response would have appeared judgmental and prideful. Christ also could have responded to them by saying, "I am now going to rebuke your selfishness by refusing to speak with you for the rest of the meal." But such an approach would have conveyed both pride and a lack of love. Instead, Jesus chose to get personally involved by correcting their error and meeting their need. He got up from the table and quietly prepared Himself to wash their feet.

C. Honesty and humility see beneath the surface (v. 5). Jesus saw the pride that was revealed by the disciples' quarreling and their unwashed feet. So He penetrated beneath the symptoms and cut right to the cause by washing His followers' feet and wiping them dry with the towel He had wrapped around His waist. Christ had that marvelous ability to hear beyond spoken words and to see behind visible acts. His authentic interest in people made it possible for Him to sense their deepest needs.

D. Honesty and humility are as comfortable receiving as they are giving (vv. 6–8a). When Jesus came to wash Simon Peter's feet, He got a hostile reception. Literally, Peter said, " 'Lord, You, my feet do You wash?' " In other words, he was saying, "Are You, Lord, going to wash my feet in front of my peers?" Peter was openly embarrassed by what Jesus was seeking to do. So in the heat of the moment, he posed a question that unveiled his pride. In fact, he eventually told Jesus, " 'Never shall You wash my feet!' " As long as Peter was giving something to someone else, his conceit remained intact. But when he was placed on the receiving end, his false humility was forced to the surface and exposed. Peter needed to learn how to receive in order to practice true humility.

E. Honesty and humility are marks of strength, not weakness (vv. 8b–10). Jesus strongly rebuked Peter's resistance. The Lord told him, " 'If I do not wash you, you have no part with Me.' " Peter then responded by asking Jesus to wash his hands and head, not just his feet. To this Christ replied, " 'He who has bathed needs only to wash his feet, but is completely clean; and you are clean.' " Jesus' love for Peter did not make Him soft and mild when it came to confronting his arrogance and extremism. The Lord corrected Peter powerfully and fairly.

F. Honesty and humility must be expressed before joy can come (vv. 12–17). After Jesus had finished washing the disciples' feet, He "reclined at the table again" and exhorted them to follow His example of servanthood. Then He added these words: " 'Truly, truly, I say to you, a slave is not greater than his master; neither is one who is sent greater than the one who sent him. If you know these things, you are blessed if you do them.' " Honesty and humility are not qualities that exist simply for the sake of discussion. They are to be actively cultivated and sincerely expressed. Then, and only then, will the everlasting happiness that comes from God be realized on earth in the lives of His people.

III. Some Crucial Questions to Answer.

If we call ourselves servants and disciples of Christ, then we must follow His example. In order to do this, we need to accurately evaluate where we are, conscientiously assess where we ought to be, and realistically plan how we can get where we should be. The following questions can help us meet these challenges to live honestly and humbly if we will take the time to answer them sincerely. Let's personalize them for the sake of application.

A. Are my words and actions prompted by love? How can I develop a greater concern for people?

B. Do I try to call attention to myself? How can I become more Christ-centered and less self-centered?

C. Am I able to compassionately surface the deep needs of others? What can I do to become more sensitive and caring?

D. **Am I a gracious receiver?** How can I become less defensive and more vulnerable in making my needs known to others?

E. **Do I really believe that honesty and humility are marks of strength?** How can I remedy my misunderstandings of these Christlike traits?

F. **Do I sincerely want the abiding joy that only God can give?** What can I do to cultivate honesty and humility so that they become natural expressions in my Christian life?

Living Insights

Study One ▬▬▬▬▬▬▬▬▬▬▬▬▬▬▬▬▬▬▬▬▬▬▬▬▬▬▬

In John 13, we see Jesus and the twelve disciples in a fascinating interchange. Here Christ is truly gentle and gracious. But notice that He is not weak or spineless! Let's delve into this challenging chapter.

- Put yourself in the scene described in John 13:1–17. Seek to feel what the disciples felt, hear what they heard, and see what they saw. Then write out these verses in *your own words.* This exercise, known as *paraphrasing,* will help you focus on the thoughts and emotions communicated in this passage.

Living Insights

Study Two ▬▬▬▬▬▬▬▬▬▬▬▬▬▬▬▬▬▬▬▬▬▬▬▬▬▬▬

Jesus' honesty and humility were unannounced. He didn't go around proclaiming, "I'm about to perform an act of humility!" On the contrary, our Lord was pleased to be unpretentious.

- How's your honesty? How are you doing in the humility department? Frankly, you may find yourself in need of some help in answering these questions. Use this "Living Insights" as an opportunity to get together with a person who knows you well. Perhaps you can meet for a meal or just a cup of coffee. When you get together, ask this person to speak straightforwardly concerning your honesty and humility. You may end up hearing some painful words. But listen to them, accept them, and take them to the Lord in prayer. Then initiate a plan of action to improve your transparency and self-perspective.

Koinōnía: Concerns and Restoration

Selected Scripture

Do you know a Christian who once walked consistently with the Lord but today is living by his own power? Do you have knowledge of a believer who has a need that is not currently being met? Chances are good that you were able to answer yes to both questions. In fact, you may have even had yourself in mind when you responded. Most of us are aware of another Christian who needs loving restoration. Consequently, as members of God's family, we need to come to grips with this knowledge and make the effort to act on it in practical ways. In this lesson we will take a big step toward discovering some of what Scripture teaches about renewing a Christian in love.

I. Some General Statements.

When we think about the biblical teaching on this subject, we are reminded of two passages that lay much of its foundation.

A. Matthew 7:12. The first statement comes from the lips of Jesus: " 'Therefore, however you want people to treat you, so treat them, for this is the Law and the Prophets.' " There are three elements of this Golden Rule that we ought to observe. First, it is a command. The Lord morally obligates us to deal with others in a certain way. Second, it contains a comparison. We are told to treat other people *in the same manner* as we would like them to treat us. And third, it presents a concise statement of the ethical teaching set forth in the Old Testament. In other words, what " 'the Law and the Prophets' " commanded regarding how God's people were to relate to both one another and unbelievers is summed up in the Golden Rule.

B. Romans 12:10a, 13. The second overall thought is conveyed through the pen of Paul: "Be devoted to one another in brotherly love; ... contributing to the needs of the saints, practicing hospitality." The Greek term for "contributing" is the present participial form of the word *koinōnéō,* which has the term *koinōnía* as its root. *Koinōnéō* means "to share in, or to have fellowship with, another." In this context Paul is exhorting us to express our love by sharing in the needs of others through overt acts of kindness and friendship.

II. Some Specific Concerns.

Now that we have these foundational statements before us, we are ready to see how they should be worked out in situations involving Christians who need restoration. We will accomplish this task by exploring three case studies that are provided for us in Scripture. Each one will show us how we can be used by God to help make a fellow believer spiritually effective again.

A. Case Study One: The Blundering Believer (Gal. 6:1–2). In this passage the Apostle Paul addresses the situation where a Christian is "caught in [a] trespass." The Greek term for *caught* means "to overtake by surprise, to overpower before one can escape." A good synonym would be *trapped*. The other term, *trespass,* speaks of the results incurred by stepping off the right path. When we take these understandings into consideration, we can see that these words describe an individual who has blundered into a period of unproductive living. They do not suggest that any obvious sin or willful disobedience is involved. Paul says that when a Christian is discovered to be in such a situation, "you who are spiritual, restore such a one in a spirit of gentleness; each one looking to yourself, lest you too be tempted." The spiritual person is not one who is unblemished, for no one except Christ has ever possessed that qualification while on earth. Rather, Paul has in mind the Christian who is living in dependence on the Holy Spirit. This kind of individual needs to reach out and lovingly repair the damage that has occurred in the life of a believer who has erred. The principle that supports this counsel is given by Paul in these words: "Bear one another's burdens, and thus fulfill the law of Christ." Earlier in his letter to the Galatians, Paul wrote, "For the whole Law is fulfilled in one word, in the statement, 'You shall love your neighbor as yourself'" (5:14). When we help carry the loads of life that oppress or depress other believers, we facilitate their restoration in Christian love.

B. Case Study Two: The Carnal Christian (James 5:19–20). James addresses a different concern. He presents us with a situation where a fellow believer has strayed from the truth. This person has willfully turned away from the clear teaching of Scripture and has become hopelessly lost in the darkness of his own sin. James implies that apart from outside help, such an individual will not find his way back to the path of spiritual growth. Consequently, a carnal Christian needs another believer

25

to turn him back to the light of God's truth. The one who performs this rescue mission will save the disobedient believer "from death, and will cover a multitude of sins" (5:20). The kind of death in view here is not everlasting separation from God, for that can only be experienced by non-Christians (see Matt. 13:49–50; 2 Thess. 1:8–9; Rev. 20:10, 15; 21:6–8). However, the death James speaks about may refer to physical death caused by God's disciplinary action (1 Cor. 11:29–32). Or he may have in mind a temporal death of fellowship with God that can occur when a Christian habitually lives in sin. Whichever the case, James' counsel is that a worldly believer can be moved back to the road toward holiness by a Christian who cares enough to get involved. When this happens, the rebel's sins can be forgiven so that restoration can be completed.

C. **Case Study Three: The Suffering Saint** (1 John 3:17–18). These verses come from the inspired pen of the Apostle John. They neither portray a blundering believer nor a carnal Christian. Instead, they present a situation where a "brother in need" is seen by another Christian who "has the world's goods" and yet "closes his heart against him." The implication is that Christians who have the ability to even partially relieve the misery of a suffering saint should seek to do so. His or her need may be emotional, physical, or financial. But whatever it is, if Christians who can assist know about the need, then they are obligated to meet it out of love. As John so clearly states, "Little children, let us not love with word or with tongue, but in deed and truth." Genuine love does all in its power to rejuvenate the weak, uplift the downcast, heal the wounded, and provide for the needy. False love says that these things should be done, but it never gets around to doing them.

III. Some Essential Steps.

Christian fellowship involves striving to meet the needs of fellow saints. If we are to see this truth actualized in our lives, then we must put into practice the following four steps. As we do this, not only will we gain greater spiritual maturity, but the other members of Christ's Church will benefit as well.

A. **Selection.** Since none of us can meet the needs of everyone, we must narrow the field of opportunities to those we can handle. The Lord will help us do this if we will commit the selection process to Him in prayer.

B. Association. Ministry cannot take place without some sort of contact. If we really desire to have a significant impact on people's lives, then we need to get involved, not stand aloof.

C. Impartation. Becoming part of a person's life requires sacrificial giving if the relationship is motivated by love. In addition, even if the help we render is never publicly acknowledged or privately appreciated, we should keep on giving. Authentic koinōnía does not look for or depend on such gratifying responses.

D. Devotion. No matter how difficult it may be for another believer to receive our help, we need to be committed to meeting his or her needs in whatever way will most benefit him or her. This does not imply that we should be obnoxiously persistent. But it does suggest that our love should be able to withstand the assaults of those who refuse to admit their need for it.

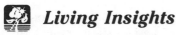 *Living Insights*

We all know Christians who once walked close to God but now are off doing their own thing. Is there a chance they could be described by one of the three categories in this study? Let's look at some biblical examples of those in need of restoration.

- Copy the following chart into your notebook. The additional Scripture texts listed below illustrate the three groups of believers mentioned in this study. After you read each passage, briefly summarize the scene presented by writing down the type of *concern* involved and the process of *restoration* needed.

Examples of Concerns and Restoration
The Blundering Believer—Galatians 2:1–16
Concern:
Restoration:
The Carnal Christian—1 Corinthians 5:1–13
Concern:
Restoration:
The Suffering Saint—James 2:14–26
Concern:
Restoration:

28

Living Insights

If we are determined to be involved in helping others, then we'll have to implement the four steps given in the lesson outline. Use the chart below to draw up tailored game plans for restoring believers who you know are blundering, carnal, or suffering. Once you have done this, commit your plans to the Lord and start putting them into practice.

Applying Restoration in Love			
Necessary Steps	Blundering Believers	Carnal Christians	Suffering Saints
Selection			
Association			
Impartation			
Devotion			

Koinōnía: Confession and Forgiveness

Selected Scripture

"We all muddle our way through a world where even well-meaning people hurt each other. When we invest ourselves in deep personal relationships, we open our souls to the wounds of another's disloyalty or even betrayal."[1] The intense hurt we experience may come from a spouse, close friend, church leader, or parent. Regardless of who inflicts it, the gash left is deep and the memories that linger are painful. If left unattended, the wound is sure to manifest itself in expressions of bitterness, anger, or guilt. But perhaps we are being one-sided about this. Are there not times when we have wielded the sword and thrust it through the spirit of another person? Have we not caused pain in the lives of others, leaving deep scars that scarcely hide emotions of resentment and thoughts of revenge? If we are honest with ourselves, most of us would have to answer yes. You see, we all sin—not just against God, but against one another as well. That's why we need to both confess our wrongs and forgive those who wrong us. Indeed, without the exercise of authentic confession and forgiveness, Christian fellowship cannot continue. The unifying bond of love is severed by believers who are at war with one another. The fighting must stop, and differences must be resolved. Exactly how can this be done? Let's find out.

I. Confession and Forgiveness Explained.

The Lord addressed this issue on at least two occasions during His earthly ministry. Both times, the counsel He gave was clear and practical. On the first occasion, Jesus specified what we should do when we have offended another person. Some time later, He spelled out how we should respond to an individual who has offended us. Let's get a handle on both sets of instruction He has given. In each, Christ presents a situation, specifies a procedure, and relays a consequence.

A. Matthew 5:23–26.
The teaching embedded in these verses forms a portion of Christ's Sermon on the Mount. For our benefit and the benefit of others, we need to heed what the Lord says here.

1. The Situation (v. 23). Jesus describes an occasion where a believer brings an offering to the altar and there remembers that he or she has offended another person.

1. Lewis B. Smedes, *Forgive and Forget: Healing the Hurts We Don't Deserve* (San Francisco: Harper and Row, 1984), p. xi.

Some historical background will help us understand what is being described here and how it relates to us. Under the Mosaic Law, a worshiper brought animals as a sacrifice to be slain on an altar before God. Through this act, he received a cleansed heart and a way of open access to the Lord. With the sacrificial death of Christ, however, the payment for sin has been made once for all (Heb. 10:10–18). Now Christians can come to God in prayer without needing another sacrifice for their sins. In light of this information, we can apply Jesus' instruction to our worship of God. As such, the scenario He is presenting concerns a situation where we come before the Lord in prayer or praise and then recall that we have deeply injured another individual.

2. The Procedure (v. 24). What should we do when this occurs? Jesus tells us in these words from Matthew 5: " 'Leave your offering there before the altar, and go your way; first be reconciled to your brother, and then come and present your offering.' " The procedure He gives is quite simple. First, we are to *stop worshiping.* Second, we are to *seek out the individual we have hurt.* And third, we are to *initiate a process of healing.* This requires that we confess the wrong, express our grief over it, and ask for forgiveness. Once this has been done, we are free to move on to the fourth step—a *return to worshiping the Lord.*

3. The Consequence (vv. 25–26). What will happen if we choose to disobey this biblical directive? Jesus does not leave us in the dark with regard to this question. He answers it in this way: " 'Make friends quickly with your opponent at law while you are with him on the way, in order that your opponent may not deliver you to the judge, and the judge to the officer, and you be thrown into prison. Truly I say to you, you shall not come out of there, until you have paid up the last cent.' " Put another way, *if we refuse to seek reconciliation with the one who has been offended by us, then we will experience a prisonlike existence.* And no release will be granted from this awful state until we confess our wrong to, and request forgiveness from, this person.

B. Matthew 18:21–35. In these verses Jesus answers a question posed by Peter. The query and response concern what we should do when someone has offended us.

1. The Situation (vv. 21–32). In Jesus' day the Pharisees taught that an offended person was obligated to forgive his offender only three times.[2] Peter wanted to know what limits Christ placed on the number of times one should forgive another, so he asked Him, " 'Lord, how often shall my brother sin against me and I forgive him? Up to seven times?' " (v. 21). Peter probably thought that this figure was very generous. But Jesus told him, " 'I do not say to you, up to seven times, but up to seventy times seven' " (v. 22). In other words, no bounds are to be placed on how often we are to forgive the offenses committed against us. Jesus used a parable to drive this point home. He told the story of a wealthy " 'king who wished to settle accounts with his slaves' " (v. 23b). One of his slaves owed him ten thousand talents (v. 24). Since a talent was probably worth a measure of gold between fifty-eight and eighty pounds, we can see that the slave was indebted to the king for several million dollars at our current rate of exchange. But because the slave could not repay the debt, the king ordered that he, his family and possessions all be sold in order to recover as much of the debt as possible (v. 25). At this announcement, the slave humbled himself before his king and begged to be granted more time to repay the money owed (v. 26). This entreaty so moved the king to compassion that he released his slave and " 'forgave him the debt' " (v. 27). Later, however, this slave encountered a second slave who owed him one hundred denarii, which is valued at sixteen to twenty dollars in today's currency and equaled an average day's wage during the time of Christ. Like the first slave, the second one was unable to pay his debt and begged for more time to come up with the deficit funds (vv. 28–29). But the slave who had been forgiven of such a huge debt refused to forgive his fellow slave for this much smaller one. Indeed, he threw the second slave in jail " 'until he should pay back what was owed' " (v. 30). When the king learned about what had transpired, he summoned his slave and said, " ' "You wicked slave, I forgave you all that debt because you entreated me" ' " (v. 32).

2. Louis A. Barbieri, Jr., "Matthew," in *The Bible Knowledge Commentary: New Testament Edition,* edited by John F. Walvoord and Roy B. Zuck (Wheaton: Victor Books, 1983), p. 62.

2. The Procedure (v. 33). The king's rhetorical response indicated what his slave should have done. " ' "Should you not also have had mercy on your fellow slave, even as I had mercy on you?" ' " Although slavery is no longer a part of our culture, the application for our day is clear. Since the divine King has forgiven us of all our sins—past, present, and future—we need to forgive those people who commit wrongs against us. After all, if we can accept God's boundless compassion toward us, how much more should we exercise compassion toward others.

3. The Consequence (vv. 34–35). But what if we choose to withhold mercy? What if we decide that we will not forgive those who have left us hurting? Jesus' words convey that the price for an unforgiving spirit will be high. He tells us this by the poignant ending He gives to the parable. He says that the king was " 'moved with anger' " over his slave's lack of compassion. So he handed his slave " 'over to the torturers until he should repay all that was owed him' " (v. 34). The Greek term for *torturers* involves the idea of plaguing or tormenting. This word is used in its verb form in other sections of Scripture to speak of a person "suffering great pain" (Matt. 8:6) and to describe the misery of a man pleading for relief in hell (Luke 16:23–24). By using this word in the closing part of the story, Christ is making His message quite clear: *When we refuse to forgive those who offend us, we will suffer torturous thoughts, miserable feelings, and agonizing unrest within.* In fact, He adds that the Heavenly Father will be the One who will hand us over to a tormenting existence if we fail to exercise forgiveness (Matt. 18:35).

II. Confession and Forgiveness Clarified.

In the Epistle of James we find a passage that succinctly summarizes and clarifies Jesus' counsel regarding confession and forgiveness. The text says, "Therefore, confess your sins to one another, and pray for one another, so that you may be healed" (James 5:16a). Let's briefly analyze its essential parts so that we will come to an accurate understanding of its meaning.

A. The Participants. The people addressed in this passage are believers who have sinned. In other words, it speaks to all Christians since all commit sin.

B. The Act. The verse exhorts God's people to confess their wrongs to one another. That is, a Christian who has hurt another Christian should go to that individual and repent. And the believer who harbors resentment against a fellow Christian should return to that person and seek reconciliation.

C. The Result. Once the offender and the offended have been brought back together, healing will take place. Those feelings of bitterness, hostility, and guilt that had festered in their lives will begin to disappear as the balm of forgiveness is applied to their wounds.

D. Some Warnings. We must be careful not to take the sound teaching in this text to an extreme. The balance we should seek can be reached if we will heed two warnings. First, we must not interpret this passage as an exhortation for Christians to confess all their sins to a local assembly of believers. The instruction here is to confess one's sin before individuals and perhaps small groups, not whole congregations. There are some matters that are inappropriate to share in front of entire church bodies. Therefore, we must always employ discretion. Second, if we do confess an offense before a group, we must be careful that our repentance does not embarrass or scandalize the individual we have hurt. Again, this problem can be avoided if we will utilize discernment.

III. Confession and Forgiveness Applied.

The Scriptures we have looked at are so important to Christian fellowship that we dare not lose the essence of their instruction and application. We can summarize the central teaching of these passages in two short statements.

1. If we have wronged someone, then we must go to that person and seek forgiveness.
2. If we harbor resentment against someone, then we must go to that person and make a confession.

The biblical counsel is clear: It makes no difference whether we are the offender or the offended—it is our responsibility to initiate the changes that can lead to the renewal of genuine koinōnía. And if we choose to withhold forgiveness, then we hurt ourselves more than we do anyone else. Lewis Smedes says it well:

Recall the pain of being wronged, the hurt of being stung, cheated, demeaned. Doesn't the memory of it fuel the fire of fury again, reheat the pain again, make it hurt again? Suppose you never forgive, suppose you feel the

34

hurt each time your memory lights on the people who did you wrong. And suppose you have a compulsion to think of them constantly. You have become a prisoner of your past pain; you are locked into a torture chamber of your own making. Time should have left your pain behind; but you keep it alive to let it flay you over and over. . . .

The only way to heal the pain that will not heal itself is to forgive the person who hurt you. Forgiving stops the reruns of pain. Forgiving heals your memory as you change your memory's vision.

When you release the wrongdoer from the wrong, you cut a malignant tumor out of your inner life.

You set a prisoner free, but you discover that the real prisoner was yourself.[3]

3. Smedes, *Forgive and Forget,* pp. 132–33.

 *Living Insights*

When it comes to confessing and forgiving, the correct procedure is often partially violated or totally ignored. Given this, let's break down piece by piece the passages we have just dealt with so that we can gain an even greater understanding of their counsel.

● Copy the following chart into your notebook. Then carefully reread the two passages from Matthew and the verse from James. After you have done this, seek to answer the questions listed below from each of the biblical texts. This process will help you get a firmer handle on the teachings they present.

Confession and Forgiveness			
Questions	Matthew 5:23–26	Matthew 18:21–35	James 5:16
Who?			
What?			
Where?			
When?			
Why?			
How?			

Living Insights

If we limit our study of koinōnía to mere academics, we've really fallen short of God's intended purpose. We must press on to the issue of application—implementing God's truth in our lives.

- Applying confession and forgiveness requires our action. Look again at the two concluding statements:

    1. If we have wronged someone, then we must go to that person and seek forgiveness.
    2. If we harbor resentment against someone, then we must go to that person and make a confession.

Which statement do you identify with? Take the time to think through them, pray about them, and most of all, *act* on them.

Koinōnía: Encouragement and Availability
Hebrews 10:1–25

Throughout time, people have reflected on certain periods of history and have wished that they could return to those "golden days." But one problem with this desire is that the good ol' days were usually not as great as they are remembered to have been. When recalling specific events from our past, we tend to forget the daily irritations and struggles, and instead we focus purely on the enjoyable moments. This practice may have benefits at times, but it is not entirely realistic. What we need to do is reflect on both the happy and sad events in our past. By doing so, we can come to a clearer knowledge of where we are and why. And we can draw some conclusions as to where we ought to be heading and how we can best get there. This treatment of the past is advocated throughout Scripture, but perhaps it is best supported in Hebrews 10:1–25. Here we find a clear appraisal of the believer's past position under the Law and the Christian's present position in Jesus Christ. As we explore these matters, we will discover that they have a practical bearing on koinōnía; they lay the theological foundation for manifesting encouragement and availability in the local church.

I. **The Believer under the Law** (Hebrews 10:1–4).

The writer of the Book of Hebrews begins this section by reminding his original readers of their forefathers' worship practices under the Mosaic Law. Let's probe into what he has to say.

A. **An Explanation of Animal Sacrifices.** God specified through Moses that believers were commanded to take certain animals to a priest as a sin offering for specific kinds of offenses. The priest would then slaughter and burn the animals in the appropriate manner, providing an avenue of atonement for those who trusted in God.

B. **Some Limitations of Animal Sacrifices.** As wonderful as this provision for the forgiveness of sin was, it had certain built-in limitations. For example, the animal sacrifices could never "make perfect those who draw near" (v. 1b). They could not make saints holy. In fact, the sacrifices served as a constant reminder that believers were sinners and that they desperately needed God's merciful grace (vv. 2–3). Furthermore, "the blood of bulls and goats" could not "take away sins" (v. 4). Animal offerings were never designed to remove the sin barrier between God and man. So what or who could do it?

II. The Savior as the Sacrifice (Hebrews 10:5–10).

Through His Son, the Lord did what animal sacrifices were incapable of accomplishing. The writer of Hebrews makes two points in this regard. First, God's eternal Son joined Himself to a sinless human body that had been prepared by His Father (v. 5; cf. Luke 1:26–38). Second, Christ did this in order to accomplish His Father's will even to the point of dying for man's sins (Heb. 10:6–10; cf. 2:14–17; John 4:34, 5:30, 6:38–40; Luke 22:41–42). Christ's death on the cross provided a sufficient sacrifice for the sins of all mankind.

III. The Christian because of the Cross (Hebrews 10:10–25).

In these verses the writer weaves the practical implications of Christ's substitutionary death at Calvary through the fabric of his argument. Let's consider what he lays before us.

A. What We Have. The same God that willed Jesus' sacrifice on the cross for man's sins has *sanctified* all of us who trust in Christ for our salvation (v. 10). This does not mean that we are now experientially sinless. But it does mean that through our faith in Christ's death we have been set apart by God and sealed forever in His Son (cf. Eph. 1:13). Consequently, the Heavenly Father views us through His Son and thereby decrees us to be positionally perfect "for all time" (Heb. 10:14). Put another way, since Christ is perfect and we are in Him, then, as far as our standing before God is concerned, we are perfect as well. The Lord knows that we still sin, but this does not negate the fact that in Christ we have been declared righteous before the bar of the impartial Judge. Furthermore, Jesus' once-for-all sacrifice has brought us *confidence* (vv. 19-20; cf. 4:16). We can now come boldly before God's throne in prayer because Christ paved the way for us through His death. In addition, we now have "a *great priest* over the house of God" (10:21, emphasis added). We do not need to gain access to God through priests, preachers, or animal sacrifices. The only Mediator between God and man is Jesus Christ (cf. 1 Tim. 2:5–6). He has opened for us a direct channel to the Creator, Sustainer, and Redeemer of all. That's terrific news!

B. What We Should Do. Based upon the sufficiency and provision of Christ's sacrifice, the writer of Hebrews gives us three imperatives.

1. **Draw near.** We are commanded to "draw near with a sincere heart in full assurance of faith, having our hearts sprinkled clean from an evil conscience and our bodies washed with pure water" (Heb. 10:22). Old Testament saints longed for the time when they could come personally and confidently into God's presence. But not until Christ died on the cross and rose from the grave did this dream become a reality. Today we can and should approach the Lord with the full assurance that He has accepted us through our faith in the shed blood of Jesus Christ.
2. **Hold fast.** We are also exhorted to "hold fast the confession of our hope without wavering, for He who promised is faithful" (v. 23). That is, we should firmly embrace the central doctrines of Christianity, realizing that God's Word and promises are reliable. If we fail to obey this command, then we will begin to drift toward the rocks of heresy and unbelief. Such a course will make our navigation through life precarious at best and deadly at worst. We need a strong commitment to Christian truth so that we can steer straight and steadily through the dangerous waters that await us.
3. **Consider how to motivate one another.** Finally, we are told to "consider how to stimulate one another to love and good deeds" (v. 24). This involves at least two actions. First, *we need to be available to one another,* "not forsaking our own assembling together" (v. 25a). We should not be isolationist in our thinking or behavior. Spiritual hermits only decrease the potential effectiveness of Christ's Church. We need the insight, gifts, and love of one another so that we can function in the way that God has designed us to. Second, *we need to be "encouraging one another"* (v. 25b, emphasis added). Rather than criticize and malign, we should seek to urge each other forward to the goal of godliness. This can be done through a number of means—such as prayer, phone calls, letters, and get-togethers. Whatever channels we use, the important point to remember is that Christian maturity is our objective, and availability and encouragement are necessary tools for meeting it. How are you going to start making more time in your schedule for serving and uplifting others? The obligation and opportunity are now; the benefits to you and those to whom you minister will last forever.

Living Insights

Study One ■

There are many Scriptures that exhort us to encourage one another. Let's take a few minutes to read just a few of them.

- Take a quick inventory of the translations and/or paraphrases that are easily accessible to you. Start with the version you're accustomed to using and read the following passages. Then, reread them in one or two other versions. This process often brings fresh insight to the meaning of the text.
    - —1 Samuel 23:14–16
    - —Proverbs 12:25, 15:23
    - —Romans 14:19
    - —Ephesians 4:29
    - —1 Thessalonians 2:10–11; 5:11, 14
    - —2 Timothy 1:15–18
    - —Hebrews 3:13, 10:1–25

 Living Insights

Study Two ■

We have been sanctified; we have confidence; we have a great Priest. Therefore, let us draw near to God, hold fast to the Christian faith, and consider how to stimulate one another to love and good deeds. Now let's put these great exhortations into action.

- The plan is simple: Think of a way to encourage another person, and then go do it! Let's focus on an individual from each of three different groups.
    - —How can I encourage someone in my *family?*
    - —How can I encourage someone in my *church?*
    - —How can I encourage someone in my *neighborhood?*

Psalm of My Life
. . . and Yours
Psalm 1

Before we raised anchor and set sail across the waters toward koinōnía, we were warned that the journey would be hazardous to our selfishness and isolationism. And so it has been. We have seen that real Christian fellowship is characterized by such personal risks as love, acceptance, honesty, humility, restoration, confession, forgiveness, encouragement, and availability. We have also discovered that these are challenges God wants us to experience, and that He rewards us for accepting them. But our voyage is not over yet. There is one more peril that we must examine before we can safely return to shore. This last danger involves a personal choice to either accept or reject God's offer of salvation. The two paths between which we must choose—the light of righteousness and the dark of wickedness—are contrasted in Psalm 1. And depending on which one we choose, either the rewards of koinōnía will be ours to enjoy, or the consequences of self-centeredness will be ours to suffer. It's not difficult to see that this is the most important decision any of us can make. So let's navigate our ships toward one final confrontation with the powerful currents surrounding authentic fellowship. If we steer them in the right direction, we will either find a new Captain at the helms of our lives or renew our trust in His ability to guide us safely through the hazards of life.

I. The Godly Person . . .

The first three verses of this ancient psalm describe what the life of a faithful believer is like. Let's examine their content in detail.

A. Is Blessed (v. 1). The psalm opens with an exclamatory statement:

> How blessed is the man who does not walk in the
> counsel of the wicked,
> Nor stand in the path of sinners,
> Nor sit in the seat of scoffers!

The Hebrew term for *blessed* is plural, and it conveys the idea of possessing many "happinesses." As such, we could bring out the meaning of the opening words in verse 1 through this paraphrase: "Oh the happiness many times over of the person who . . ." What is it that brings an individual such a great abundance of joy? The psalmist provides the answer in three negative statements that communicate one positive truth— namely, that *from the uncompromising purity of a righteous walk*

42

with God flows a life of ever-abounding joy. Let's briefly examine each of the negative statements.

1. **He does not "walk in the counsel of the wicked."** The Hebrew word translated *walk* suggests the idea of casually moving along a chosen path. In this context, it refers to a person who does not even flirt with adopting the philosophies of the wicked.

2. **He does not "stand in the path of sinners."** The Hebrew term for *path* literally means "way." It refers to a manner in which something or someone behaves (cf. Prov. 30:18–20). In Psalm 1:1, this word is used to describe an individual who chooses not to follow the practices of the ungodly.

3. **He does not "sit in the seat of scoffers."** The idea conveyed by the Hebrew word for *sit* is a permanent settling down or dwelling in a particular place. The psalmist uses this word to denote a person who refuses to adhere to the attitudes of the blasphemous. In short, *the genuinely happy individual is the one who conforms to God's standard of righteousness rather than to the world's bent toward wickedness.*

B. Is Occupied with God's Word (v. 2). Beginning in this verse, the psalmist turns to a more positive statement on the godly life. He says of the faithful saint, "his delight is in the law of the Lord, / And in His law he meditates day and night." The Scriptures direct our steps toward holiness, not sinfulness. If we are going to travel God's way, then we must follow the principles presented in His Word. When we do, we will find satisfaction. But we cannot live according to the Bible without consistently spending time pondering its content and application to our lives.

C. Will Become Like a Tree (v. 3). The individual who avoids the way of the wicked and meditates on the Word of God "will be like a tree." The psalmist gives four characteristics of a tree that graphically illustrate the life of the godly. First, *the righteous person will find himself "firmly planted by streams of water"* (v. 3a). The refreshing springs of God's Word will bring nourishment to his life and thereby make it stable and strong. Second, *he will yield fruit in the proper season* (v. 3b). As he becomes more consistent in his spiritual growth, he will produce more God-honoring works. Third, *the faithful believer will bear leaves that do "not wither"* (v. 3c). When the harsh winds and crippling droughts of life come, he will stand undaunted and even continue to grow unhindered (cf. Jer. 17:8). And fourth, *"in whatever he does,"* he will *prosper* (Ps. 1:3d). The Lord will reward his faithfulness by empowering him to fulfill the lifetime goals that He has designed for him. What better success could anyone hope for!

II. The Ungodly Person . . .

In contrast to the way of the righteous is the way of the wicked. Let's consider what the inspired psalmist says about the unrighteous and compare it with the description he gives of the righteous.

A. **Is Not Like the Godly** (v. 4a). The writer begins the contrast with these abrupt words: "The wicked are not so." Who are the wicked not like? They are unlike the righteous who are happy many times over. The ungodly do not delight in or meditate on God's Word. Neither are they like a tree—strong and productive. Then to what can unbelievers be compared?

B. **Is Like Worthless Chaff** (v. 4b). We are told that the wicked are "like chaff which the wind drives away." Chaff is the outer part of the seed or grain that falls away during the threshing process. During Old Testament times, threshing floors were "usually placed on high ground to take advantage of every breeze." As "the corn was threshed out and winnowed by throwing it up against the wind with shovels, the grain [would fall] on the floor to be carefully gathered up, [and] the chaff [was] left to be carried away by the wind and vanish."[1] The psalmist uses this imagery to say that the character of unbelievers is worthless and that their fate is one of uselessness and destruction. How different a picture this is from the portrait of the believer!

C. **Will Not Share the Destiny of the Godly** (vv. 5–6). Because the wicked are lacking a righteous foundation and lifestyle, they "will not stand in the judgment" (v. 5a). That is, when they are brought before the bar of divine justice, they will be utterly unable to endure God's impartial decision. Any excuse or defense they may offer will collapse under the weight of the evidence that will be mounted against them. Rather than standing defiantly before God, they will fall to their knees and

1. A. F. Kirkpatrick, *The Book of Psalms,* Thornapple Commentaries (Grand Rapids: Baker Book House, reprint, 1902), p. 4.

confess with their lips that Jesus Christ is Lord (cf. Phil. 2:9–11). Furthermore, "sinners [will not stand] in the assembly of the righteous" (Ps. 1:5b). One facet of God's final judgment will be the separation of wheat from tares, grain from chaff—believers from unbelievers (cf. Matt. 3:12; 13:24–30, 36–43). The reason the ungodly will be convicted and expelled by God's judgment is that "the Lord knows the way of the righteous, / But the way of the wicked will perish" (Ps. 1:6). God's special love for believers will not allow Him to grant unbelievers the same destiny He has granted His children. Thus, while the godly life leads to prosperity and everlasting joy through communion with God, the ungodly life leads to ruin and everlasting despair through separation from God (v. 6b; cf. 2 Thess. 1:6–10, 1 Pet. 1:3–9, Rev. 20:10–22:5).

III. The Parting of the Ways.

The psalmist indicates that there are two courses we can take in life. We can walk down the path of either wickedness or righteousness. The former course brings a valueless existence and an everlasting death. The latter path brings both a worthwhile existence and an everlasting life. There is no middle road or third way. In fact, all those who have not placed their faith in God through Jesus Christ *are* trodding the way of the wicked. Are *you* on this road? If so, then realize that you do not have to stay on it. Regardless of your past or present, you are welcome to lock arms with God through His Son and walk in righteousness forever with Him. On the other hand, if you are already a believer in Christ, then continue to walk in the grace you have received. The goal of salvation is the purification and glorification of saints (Rom. 8:30, Jude 24). Are you striving to be Christlike in your thoughts and deeds? Or are you flirting with the way of the wicked? In either case, realize that your enjoyment of the full benefits of genuine koinōnía is dependent on your abhorring what is evil and clinging to what is good (Rom. 12:9–10). The superabundant joy that only God can give awaits you. And the only prerequisites are that you place your faith in His Son and walk consistently in His way. Will you make these commitments today?

Living Insights

The Word of God clearly states the need for koinōnía—Christian fellowship. Throughout our study, we found passages in the Gospels, Acts, and Epistles that dealt with this subject. We even discovered some timeless counsel embedded in a wisdom psalm from the Old Testament. Since we have covered so much ground, let's use our final set of "Living Insights" to review some of the riches we have unearthed.

• After you've made a copy of the following chart in your notebook, look back through your notes and study guide. As you do, zero in on one scriptural truth that you found to be especially significant from each lesson.

Koinōnía: Authentic Fellowship	
Lesson Titles	Significant Truths
Koinōnía	
Koinōnía: Love and Acceptance	
Koinōnía: Love, Sweet Love	
Koinōnía: Honesty and Humility	
Koinōnía: Concerns and Restoration	
Koinōnía: Confession and Forgiveness	
Koinōnía: Encouragement and Availability	
Psalm of My Life . . . and Yours	

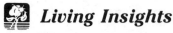 *Living Insights*

Koinōnía is a noun with the qualities of a verb. It's a word of action! Hopefully, the message of involvement it conveys has come through loud and clear in this series. But just so we don't miss it, let's retrace our steps through the numerous applications we've made together.

- The following chart is identical to the previous one, with a single exception. This chart emphasizes a review of *meaningful applications,* not significant truths. So as you review your notes, jot down in the right column the most important application that you made from each lesson. Then continue in God's power to flesh them out in your life.

Koinōnía: Authentic Fellowship	
Lesson Titles	Meaningful Applications
Koinōnía	
Koinōnía: Love and Acceptance	
Koinōnía: Love, Sweet Love	
Koinōnía: Honesty and Humility	
Koinōnía: Concerns and Restoration	
Koinōnía: Confession and Forgiveness	
Koinōnía: Encouragement and Availability	
Psalm of My Life . . . and Yours	

Books for Probing Further

Our voyage is complete ... or is it? Certainly we have a much better idea of the nature and risks of genuine fellowship than we had when we first embarked on our journey. And we have begun to experience the joys of koinōnía as we have sought to encourage its development in our lives. Now that we're back on shore, the path of consistent appropriation stretches out before us, beckoning us to keep moving forward. But this involves having the right tools at our disposal. Fortunately, there are several excellent books that can serve as valuable resources for our travels on the road of application. Of the many books we could name, the following have been selected because they are founded in Scripture, committed to clear communication, and focused on relevant application. If you would like to explore more fully the rich landscape of koinōnía and become equipped more thoroughly to enjoy its fruits, then we would encourage you to consult the sources we have listed below. But remember, these books are given as aids, not substitutes, for your experience of Christian fellowship.

I. Fellowship through Service.

The basic manifestation of true koinōnía is service to others. These materials will provide you with practical instruction on how to help others biblically and effectively.

Berry, Jo. *Growing, Sharing, Serving.* Elgin: David C. Cook Publishing Co., 1979.

Bridges, Jerry. *True Fellowship.* The Christian Character Library. Colorado Springs: NavPress, 1985.

Getz, Gene A. *Serving One Another.* Wheaton: Victor Books, 1984.

Little, Paul. *How to Give Away Your Life.* Foreword by Marie Little. Santa Ana: Vision House, 1978.

MacDonald, Gail and Gordon. *If Those Who Reach Could Touch.* Chicago: Moody Press, 1984.

Stedman, Ray C. *Body Life.* Foreword by Billy Graham. Glendale: Regal Books, 1972.

Swindoll, Charles R. *Improving Your Serve: The Art of Unselfish Living.* Waco: Word Books, 1981.

Wilke, Harold H. *Creating the Caring Congregation.* Foreword by Dr. Karl A. Menninger. Nashville: Abingdon Press, 1980.

Williams, June A. *Strategy of Service.* Ministers Resource Library. Grand Rapids: Zondervan Publishing House, 1984.

Wilson, Earl D. *Loving Enough to Care.* Portland: Multnomah Press, 1984.

Yagel, Bobbie. *Living with Yourself and Other Imperfect People.* Grand Rapids: Chosen Books, the Zondervan Corporation, 1983.

II. Fellowship through Love and Acceptance.

Our ability to love and accept others is intricately related to our self-perspective (Matt. 22:39, Eph. 5:28–29). Because of this, we have listed a number of books that deal not only with the art of loving others but also with our need to love ourselves.

Aldrich, Joseph C. *Love for All Your Worth: A Quest for Personal Value and Lovability.* Portland: Multnomah Press, 1985.

Aldrich, Joseph C. *Self-worth: How to Become More Loveable.* Portland: Multnomah Press, 1982.

Baker, Don. *Acceptance: Loosing the Webs of Personal Insecurity.* Portland: Multnomah Press, 1985.

Hocking, David L. *Who Am I? And What Difference Does It Make?* Portland: Multnomah Press, 1985.

Kelsey, Morton T. *Caring: How Can We Love One Another?* New York: Paulist Press, 1981.

Keyes, Dick. *Beyond Identity: Finding Yourself in the Image and Character of God.* Foreword by William Kirk Kilpatrick. Ann Arbor: Servant Books, 1984.

Lewis, C. S. *The Four Loves.* New York: Harcourt Brace Jovanovich, 1960.

McDowell, Josh. *His Image, My Image.* Foreword by Lawrence J. Crabb, Jr. San Bernardino: Here's Life Publishers, Inc., 1984.

McDowell, Josh. *The Secret of Loving: How a Lasting Intimate Relationship Can Be Yours.* San Bernardino: Here's Life Publishers, Inc., 1985.

Smith, M. Blaine. *One of a Kind: A Biblical View of Self-acceptance.* Downers Grove: InterVarsity Press, 1984.

Ward, Ruth McRoberts. *Self-esteem: Gift from God.* Foreword by Cecil G. Osborne. Grand Rapids: Baker Book House, 1984.

Wulf, Dick. *Find Yourself, Give Yourself.* Colorado Springs: NavPress, 1983.

Yohn, Rick. *Beyond Spiritual Gifts.* Wheaton: Tyndale House Publishers, Inc., 1976.

III. Fellowship through Honesty and Humility.

Truthfulness, vulnerability, tactfulness, and humility are essential for the development of authentic koinōnía. But how can these traits become part of our everyday lives? The following works will help you answer this relevant question.

Augsburger, David. *When Caring Is Not Enough: Resolving Conflicts through Fair Fighting.* Ventura: Regal Books, 1983.

Howard, J. Grant. *The Trauma of Transparency: A Biblical Approach to Inter-Personal Communication.* A Critical Concern Book. Portland: Multnomah Press, 1979.

Huggett, Joyce. *Creative Conflict: How to Confront and Stay Friends.* Downers Grove: InterVarsity Press, 1984.

Swindoll, Charles R. *Dropping Your Guard: The Value of Open Relationships.* Waco: Word Books, 1983.

Swindoll, Charles R. *Integrity: The Mark of Godliness.* Portland: Multnomah Press, 1981.

IV. Fellowship through Restoration.

Perhaps the most difficult task of koinōnía is restoring a fellow believer who is blundering, carnal, or suffering. And once a Christian has been returned to righteous living, he or she needs to learn how to better handle temptation and be encouraged to continue toward holiness. In recent years, a number of books on this topic have been published. Here you will find a listing of several that deal sensitively with these concerns.

Alcorn, Randy C. *Christians in the Wake of the Sexual Revolution: Recovering Our Sexual Sanity.* A Critical Concern Book. Portland: Multnomah Press, 1985.

Baker, Don. *Beyond Forgiveness: The Healing Touch of Church Discipline.* Portland: Multnomah Press, 1984.

Baker, Don. *Beyond Rejection: The Church, Homosexuality and Hope.* Foreword by Frank Worthen. Portland: Multnomah Press, 1985.

Bridges, Jerry. *The Pursuit of Holiness.* Colorado Springs: NavPress, 1978.

Busséll, Harold L. *Lord, I Can Resist Anything but Temptation.* Grand Rapids: Pyranee Books, Zondervan Publishing House, 1985.

Cerling, Charles, Jr. *Freedom from Bad Habits.* San Bernardino: Here's Life Publishers, Inc., 1984.

Gage, Ken and Joy. *Restoring Fellowship.* Chicago: Moody Press, 1984.

Kehl, D. G. *Control Yourself! Practicing the Art of Self-discipline.* Grand Rapids: Zondervan Publishing House, 1982.

Lutzer, Erwin W. *How to Say No to a Stubborn Habit—Even When You Feel like Saying Yes.* Foreword by Stuart Briscoe. Wheaton: Victor Books, 1979.

Lutzer, Erwin W. *How in This World Can I Be Holy?* Chicago: Moody Press, 1985.

Lutzer, Erwin W. *Living with Your Passions.* Foreword by Josh McDowell. Critical Issues Series. Wheaton: Victor Books, 1983.

Lutzer, Erwin W. *When a Good Man Falls.* Wheaton: Victor Books, 1985.

Merrill, Dean. *Another Chance: How God Overrides Our Big Mistakes.* Grand Rapids: Zondervan Publishing House, 1981.

Swindoll, Charles R. *Moral Purity.* Fullerton: Insight for Living, 1985.

Swindoll, Charles R. *Sensuality: Resisting the Lure of Lust.* Portland: Multnomah Press, 1981.

Swindoll, Charles R. *Starting Over: Fresh Hope for the Road Ahead.* Portland: Multnomah Press, 1977.

Tournier, Paul. *The Healing of Persons.* Foreword by Georges Bickel. Translated by Edwin Hudson. San Francisco: Harper and Row, 1965.

Weese, Wightman. *Back in Touch.* Wheaton: Tyndale House, 1984.

White, John, and Blue, Ken. *Healing the Wounded: The Costly Love of Church Discipline.* Foreword by Ray C. Stedman. Downers Grove: InterVarsity Press, 1985.

Wilson, Earl D. *Sexual Sanity: Breaking Free from Uncontrolled Habits.* Downers Grove: InterVarsity Press, 1984.

V. Fellowship through Confession and Forgiveness.

In our imperfect, sin-ridden world, there will be times when we offend each other. Occasions such as these call for reconciliation. Without this response, wounds will fester and resentment will intensify. The sources listed below can help you apply the healing balm of confession and forgiveness.

Augsburger, David. *Caring Enough to Forgive.* Ventura: Regal Books, 1981.

Augsburger, David. *The Freedom of Forgiveness: Seventy Times Seven.* Chicago: Moody Press, 1970.

Davis, Ron Lee. *A Forgiving God in an Unforgiving World.* With James D. Denney. Foreword by Bruce Larson. Eugene: Harvest House Publishers, 1984.

Evans, Colleen Townsend. *Start Loving, Keep Loving: The Miracle of Forgiving.* Rev. ed. Garden City: Doubleday and Co., Inc., 1985.

Hembree, Ron. *The Speck in Your Brother's Eye.* Old Tappan: Fleming H. Revell Co., 1985.

Lutzer, Erwin W. *Failure: The Back Door to Success.* Chicago: Moody Press, 1975.

Mains, Karen Burton. *The Key to an Open Heart.* Elgin: David C. Cook Publishing Co., 1979.

Murray, Andrew. *Confession: The Road to Forgiveness.* Springdale: Whitaker House, 1983.

Nystrom, Carolyn. *Why Do I Do Things Wrong?* Illustrated by Wayne A. Hanna. Children's Bible Basics. Chicago: Moody Press, 1981.

Smedes, Lewis B. *Forgive and Forget: Healing the Hurts We Don't Deserve.* San Francisco: Harper and Row, 1984.

VI. Fellowship through Encouragement and Availability.

If we really desire to serve people, then we will seek to develop and maintain caring relationships. But this goal cannot be accomplished unless we are available to meet needs and are encouraging in our responses. These sources will provide you with some valuable counsel on how to do this.

Briscoe, Jill, and Golz, Judy. *Space to Breathe, Room to Grow.* Nashville: Oliver-Nelson Books, Thomas Nelson Publishers, 1985.

Collins, Gary, Dr. *How to Be a People Helper.* Santa Ana: Vision House, 1976.

Crabb, Lawrence J., Jr., and Allender, Dan B. *Encouragement: The Key to Caring.* Grand Rapids: Zondervan Publishing House, 1984.

Doering, Jeanne. *Your Power of Encouragement.* Chicago: Moody Press, 1982.

Hilt, James. *How to Have a Better Relationship with Anybody: A Biblical Approach.* Chicago: Moody Press, 1984.

Inrig, Gary. *Quality Friendship: The Risks and Rewards.* Foreword by Erwin W. Lutzer. Chicago: Moody Press, 1981.

McMinn, Gordon. *Choosing to Be Close: Fill Your Life with Rewarding Relationships.* Portland: Multnomah Press, 1984.

Narramore, Kathy, and Hill, Alice. *Kindred Spirits: Developing Godly Friendships.* Grand Rapids: Pyranee Books, Zondervan Publishing House, 1985.

Reeve, Pamela. *Relationships: What It Takes to Be a Friend.* Portland: Multnomah Press, 1982.

Smith, David W. *The Friendless American Male.* Foreword by Jim Conway. Ventura: Regal Books, 1983.

Strauss, Richard. *Getting Along with Each Other.* San Bernardino: Here's Life Publishers, Inc., 1985.

Swindoll, Charles R. *Encourage Me.* Portland: Multnomah Press, 1982.

White, Jerry and Mary. *Friends and Friendship: The Secrets of Drawing Closer.* Colorado Springs: NavPress, 1982.

Wiersbe, Warren W. *Be Encouraged.* Wheaton: Victor Books, 1984.

Insight for Living
Cassette Tapes
Koinōnía

We really do need each other. God made us that way! The ancient Greeks called this fellowship *koinōnía* . . . a concept that is especially relevant in our self-sufficient age. This series of biblical expositions spells out the particulars involved in changing your relationships with others from superficial and shallow to compassionate and caring. You will find these principles helpful in breaking down walls of prejudice that keep us from knowing and loving one another.

U.S.	**Cassette series—includes album cover**	**$23.75**
KOI CS	**Individual cassettes—include messages**	
	A and B	**5.00**
Canadian	**Cassette series—includes album cover**	**30.00**
KOI CS	**Individual cassettes—include messages**	
	A and B	**6.35**

These prices are effective as of November 1985 and are subject to change.

KOI 1-A: *Koinōnía*
            Acts 2:44–47
     B: *Koinōnía: Love and Acceptance*
            1 Corinthians 13:1–5a

KOI 2-A: *Koinōnía: Love, Sweet Love*
            1 Corinthians 13:5b–7
     B: *Koinōnía: Honesty and Humility*
            Luke 22:7–14, 23–24; John 13:1–17

KOI 3-A: *Koinōnía: Concerns and Restoration*
            Selected Scripture
     B: *Koinōnía: Confession and Forgiveness*
            Selected Scripture

KOI 4-A: *Koinōnía: Encouragement and Availability*
            Hebrews 10:1–25
     B: *Psalm of My Life . . . and Yours**
            Psalm 1

*This message was not a part of the original series but is compatible with it.

Ordering Information

Payment Options: We accept personal checks, money orders, Visa, and MasterCard in payment for materials ordered. Unfortunately, we are unable to offer invoicing or COD orders. If the amount of your check or money order is less than the amount of your purchase, your check will be returned so that you may place your order again with the correct amount. All orders must be paid in full before shipment can be made.

U.S. Ordering Information: You are welcome to use our toll-free number (for orders only) between the hours of 8:30 A.M. and 4:00 P.M., Pacific Time, Monday through Friday. We can accept only Visa or MasterCard when ordering by phone. The number is (800) 772-8888. This number may be used anywhere in the continental United States excluding California, Hawaii, and Alaska. Orders from those areas are handled through our Sales Department at (714) 870-9161. We are unable to accept collect calls.

Your order will be processed promptly. We ask that you allow four to six weeks for delivery by fourth-class mail. If you wish your order to be shipped first-class, please add 10 percent of the total order (not including California sales tax) for shipping and handling.

Canadian Ordering Information: Your order will be processed promptly. We ask that you allow approximately four weeks for delivery by first-class mail to the U.S./Canadian border. All orders will be shipped from our office in Fullerton, California. For our listeners in British Columbia, a 7 percent sales tax must be added to the total of all tape orders (not including first-class postage). For further information, please contact our office at (604) 669-1916.

Returned Checks: There is a $10 charge for any returned check (regardless of the amount of your order) to cover processing and invoicing.

Guarantee: Our tapes are guaranteed for ninety days against faulty performance or breakage due to a defect in the tape. For best results, please be sure your tape recorder is in good operating condition and is cleaned regularly.

Mail your order to one of the following addresses:

Insight for Living
Sales Department
Post Office Box 4444
Fullerton, CA 92634

Insight for Living Ministries
Post Office Box 2510
Vancouver, BC
Canada V6B 3W7

Quantity discounts and gift certificates are available upon request.

Overseas ordering information is provided on the reverse side of the order form.

Order Form

Please send me the following cassette tapes:

The current series: ☐ KOI CS Koinōnía: Authentic Fellowship
Individual tapes: ☐ KOI 1 ☐ KOI 2 ☐ KOI 3 ☐ KOI 4

I am enclosing:

$_____ To purchase cassette series for $23.75 (in Canada $30.00*) which includes the album cover

$_____ To purchase individual cassettes at $5.00 each (in Canada $6.35*)

$_____ Total of purchases

$_____ California residents please add 6 percent sales tax

$_____ *British Columbia residents please add 7 percent sales tax

$_____ Canadian residents please add 6 percent for postage

$_____ U.S. residents please add 10 percent for first-class shipping and handling if desired

$_____ **Overseas residents please add appropriate postage**
(See postage chart under "Overseas Ordering Information.")

$_____ Gift for the Insight for Living radio ministry for which a tax-deductible receipt will be issued

$_____ **Total Amount Due (please do not send cash)**

Form of payment:
☐ *Check or money order made payable to Insight for Living*
☐ *Credit card (VISA or MasterCard only)*
If there is a balance: ☐ *Apply it as a donation* ☐ *Please refund*

Credit Card Purchases:
☐ *VISA* ☐ *MasterCard Number* _____
Expiration Date _____
Signature _____
   We cannot process your credit card purchase without your signature.

Name _____

Address _____

_____

City _____ *Radio Station* _____

State/Province _____ *Zip/Postal Code* _____

Country _____

Telephone (   ) _____
   Should questions arise concerning your order, we may need to contact you.

Overseas Ordering Information

In order for us to process your request, please read the following instructions carefully. We ask that you allow approximately twelve to sixteen weeks for delivery by surface mail. If you would like your order sent airmail, the length of delivery may be reduced. All orders will be shipped from our office in Fullerton, California.

Payment Options: We can accept personal checks made payable in U.S. funds, international money orders, Visa, and MasterCard in payment for materials ordered. This request is necessary due to fluctuating currency rates. If the amount of your check or money order is less than the amount of your purchase, your check will be returned so that you may place your order again with the correct amount. All orders must be paid in full before shipment can be made.

Postage and Handling: Please add to the amount purchased the basic postage cost for the service you desire. All orders must include postage based on the chart below.

Purchase Amount		Surface Postage	Airmail Postage
From	To	Percent of Order	Percent of Order
$ .01	$15.00	40%	75%
15.01	75.00	25%	45%
75.01	or more	15%	40%

Returned Checks: There is a $10 charge for any returned check (regardless of the amount of your order) to cover processing and invoicing.

Guarantee: Our tapes are guaranteed for ninety days against faulty performance or breakage due to a defect in the tape. For best results, please be sure your tape recorder is in good operating condition and is cleaned regularly.

Mail your order or inquiry to the following address:

Insight for Living
Sales Department
Post Office Box 4444
Fullerton, CA 92634

Quantity discounts and gift certificates are available upon request.